you CAN SEE

*"What will you do if you knew
you could see your tomorrow, now?"*

MOSES A. IYAMU

You Can See
By Moses Airen Iyamu

© 2020

This book cannot be distributed by any electronic or mechanical means, in print or online. No part of it may be altered, reproduced or downloaded without the express written permission of the author.

All Bible references taken from King James Version

Published by:
Mountchris Venturees
19, Ogunnipebi Street,
Off Akilo Road, Ogba Ikeja
Lagos Nigeria
Tel: +234 (0)0807 796 5664
E-mail:udosir@gmail.com
www.mountchris.com

A Testimony City Media Publications
Tel: +234 (0) 806 401 1858
Email: testimonycitymedia99@gmail.com,
        aireniyamu@gmail.com
        https://www.facebook.com/testimonycitymedia
        www. testimonycitymedia.com

A Testimonycitymedia 2020
©testimonycitymediapublication2020

Designed & Printed by:
ALFATOA Communications
1, Boyle Street, Shomolu, Lagos
Tel: +234 - (0) 803 409 3699

©Moses Airen Iyamu   © 2020

ISBN 978 978 984 613 9

Dedication

TO my parent's grand-children, "Lord, your kingdom come in their hearts, and your will be done on earth in their Lives, just as it is already done in heaven, amen

Table of Content

Acknowledgement

The entire members and staff of testimony ministry and media. Lord, your counsel stands.

Introduction

FRIENDSHIP with man is all that God desires – Friendship. The only way you can see your tomorrow, NOW, is not through the help of a prophet, or a witch doctor, or even your pastor, but through fellowship that leads to friendship with God.

God's desire is that we know where we are coming from and where He is leading us to, according to the counsel of HIS OWN WILL (Ephesians 1:11). To experience, enjoy and fulfil God's will (plans or purpose) for our lives is the greatest adventure a man can ever have on earth, and the only way to experience this adventure is to first know His purpose for our lives.

When God first met Abraham, all He did was to invite Abraham for an adventure of his life at the age of 75 years, when, to Abraham, there was nothing left in life to explore. But unknown to Abraham, life was just beginning and because he believed God, he was called a friend of God.

Everyone in the bible that followed God's plans for their lives were called God's friends, because they believed Him… and this alone, pleased God (Hebrews 11:1-6).

When Jesus came, He also had friends, who were called the twelve disciples. When He was leaving the earth, He gave this command to anyone who would dare to follow Him in John 15:12-16, verse 14-15 says,

> **"Ye are my friends if you do whatsoever I command you, henceforth I call you not servants; for the servants knoweth not what his lord doeth, but I have called you friends, for all things I have heard of my Father, I have made known unto you".**

Boy! What glorious words – **"you are My friends if you do whatsoever I command you".**

Abraham was God's friend (Genesis 18:17) because he did what God told him to. What did God tell Abraham? Isaiah 51:2 says:

"God called him and told him to leave and come follow Me and I will show you a land"

Genesis 12:1

And Abraham obeyed. Moses in Exodus 33:11 was also called "friend". Today, Jesus through the Holy Spirit is saying the same things he said to Abraham (in John 3:3-6) which says:

"Verily, verily, I say unto thee, except a man be born again, he cannot SEE the kingdom of God". "Verily, verily I say unto thee, except a man be born of water (Which means the WORD)

– Ephesians 5:25 -26

And of the Spirit, (John 1:11-13) he cannot **ENTER** into the kingdom of God.

"That which is born of the flesh is flesh (sexual intercourse), **that which is born of the Spirit is spirit** (faith)".

So, my friend, God has a land kept for you and that land, like the Garden of Eden is preserved for only you to come and keep.

WHAT YOU CAN'T SEE, YOU CAN'T ENTER... YOU NEED THE HOLY SPIRIT.

Life is so much fun if you can always see and tell what tomorrow will hold for you, or what to do next in every given or difficult situation in life.

Chapter One

You Can See

LIFE is so much fun if you can always see and tell what tomorrow will hold for you. Or what to do next in every given or difficult situation in life.

People always wonder what tomorrow holds for them and many run to find this out in the wrong place. The safest and indeed, only place to find this out is in the word of God.

Like the title goes, **You Can See** your tomorrow, today.

God, when he made man (Adam) in the beginning, showed him his purpose on earth so that man would not just be on earth doing nothing. So also did God carve out a plan for you before he allowed your father to release you into the woman or mother that carried you for nine months. You were born for a reason. You came for a definite plan on earth. You are not a mistake on earth. God, before creation had planned your place on earth and you were equipped for the work on earth. The reason you don't know or can't see it is because you are not connected to God your source and sustainer. Only God knows why you are here and only He can take you into your purpose on earth. Your father, mother, education, degree, or anything that is man-made or born of man can never take you into your purpose on earth.

When God made Adam, only God could tell where Adam could and should function well; only God could say what Adam could, and could not do on earth, and when Adam disobeyed and worked against God's plan for his life, he fell from his place of glory, his place of power with God over the affairs of the world and became subject to the influence of the affairs of what he once ruled over.

No matter how successful you are in this world or whatever you control or own if you are not doing what God created you to do, you are just exercising power in the wrong direction.

If you can understand the difference between ambition and purpose you will see that an ambitious man is very different from one with a purpose from God on earth. **explain

Some years ago, in 1995, I got admission into the

University of Agriculture, Makurdi to study Agriculture and Mathematics.

On a particular day, during our registration process, a guy spoke out while we were all waiting to enrol and said that as he stood, God had shown him his end (how he would die) as a believer, and his end if he should backslide. I don't know how many people heard him that day but those words changed my life forever. I am still living on those words I heard in 1995. I went to my hotel room (we were not yet given permission to move into the school hostels) and went straight down on my knees to tell God about the boy I met earlier. I talked to God about how He showed him the end of his life from his beginning, while I didn't even know my beginning from my end even though I was born again at that time.

Well, I did not get the admission but I got something better than an admission - I got what most believers did not know and what some still do not know. The difference between purpose and ambition. Well, I came back to Benin and told my father what happened in the school but could not tell him what truth had been given to me because I knew he could not take it. It took me almost 7 years to begin to understand what was spoken to me that day.

Please it's not a revelation, it's just the plain simple truth that God expects his people to be used to, but unfortunately, many still do not know and that's why life deals with them and they wonder if God is not seeing them.

Now follow me as we go into the word of God and back to the beginning where life first started and see whether this truth will be there. Let us also go through the pages of bible history up to this present day.

In Genesis 1:26-27, we see God creating man in his own image and after His own likeness. That means whatsoever is in God is also in man because like gives birth to like. Then God begins to say some things to the man he created, things like **'have dominion over everything'**, **'subdue and replenish the earth'** and **'multiply and fill the earth'**. After speaking to the man he made in the spirit in Genesis chapter 2, He comes to the earth and begins to mold dust from the ground and from the dust he erected a statue and breathed into that statue the spirit he created in Genesis 1:26 and then the Bible says that dust became a living thing.

John 4:24 says:

> **"God is Spirit and they that worship must worship with the help of his Spirit in us".**

So if God is Spirit, it means when He first created man in Genesis 1:26, He created a spirit and when He finished moulding the dust from the ground in Genesis 2, that dust was not man. It is just like when someone you knew died, all that was left was just an empty body (dust) lying inside the casket. The real man (which is spirit) had gone. So you see that you are a spirit put in a body.

No matter the colour of the body you are wearing, it's all dust. **THE REAL YOU IS THE MAN INSIDE.**

The assignment is both spiritual and physical. Now, why did I say that? It is because you are a spirit living in a physical world to fulfil a spiritual work using a physical body to relate with the physical things of this world. Now let me explain, what I am talking about. Adam was made in the spirit by God to come to earth and fulfil a purpose, even though he was told the purpose in the spirit before he was ever made in the physical. But because his assignment was both spiritual (because the garden of God was spiritual) but yet physical, Adam had to operate from the spiritual with God's help to rule the physical.

That's why he could name the animals on land, in the sea and air without falling sick or feeling tired after a hard day's job like people would say. The bible said that Adam did not experience anything like tiredness or sweat. All this came after the fall in the garden. We sweat and get tired or fall sick when we over work the body. But for Adam he never knew what it felt to be tired, he was fulfilling his purpose by the ability of God in him and when sin came on him that ability was lost (Genesis 3:17-19) until men began to seek God again and work with Him by faith in what He told them to do on earth for Him.

All that happened to Adam was foretold to him by God (Genesis 2:16-17) this means that whether Adam was going to fall or not, was not new to God. That is why He is called the ALL WISE ONE (1 Timothy 1:17). Of what good will God be to mankind if He cannot tell what will happen not just tomorrow but the future?

So let's see if we can find other cases like this in the bible to prove whether God really knows tomorrow.

People always wonder what tomorrow holds for them and many run to find this out in the wrong place.

Chapter Two

Men of Old

Amos 3: 7

AFTER Adam, the next man on the scene was Enoch in Genesis 5:18-24. Here, you find a man that Paul says in Hebrews 11:5:

> **"BY FAITH Enoch was translated that he should not see death: and was not found, because God had translated him: for before his translation he had this testimony, that he pleased God".**

Jude also said something about this man in his book Jude 1:14

> **"..and Enoch also, the seventh from Adam, prophesied these, saying, behold the Lord**

cometh with a thousand of His saints".

Now you may not understand what Jude is trying to say here. Let me try to paint the picture for you. Jude talked about Enoch, the man that did not see death because God took him in Genesis 5:18-24. Jude says Enoch was the seventh generation from Adam and during one of his days on earth, while he was worshipping, God revealed to/told him what was going to happen almost seven thousand years later. I mean when God was talking to Enoch (and the man was just seven generations from Adam and maybe he even saw Adam or maybe not). But the fall of Adam was still fresh in the air.

Then see what God did to this man, instead of telling him what was needful for his days - He began to tell him what will happen not during Noah's time, nor during Abraham, nor during Moses, not even that Jesus will be born but that Jesus will come with ten thousand of his saints to judge the earth. And you and I are waiting for that day because the Jesus that Enoch saw coming, we read that he came and that he said he would come again (Acts 1:10-11). But God told someone about this even before the tribe of Israel was ever founded by Jacob! Centuries before science and technology and whatever you can now think of had ever happened in this world.

God bypassed all this and even things happening now

that you are reading this book, and told Enoch what will happen in our time that had no relevance to him and his generation. Why am I showing you this? You may ask. The reason is that God delights to show His children events before they happen, so that men may fear Him (Isaiah 41:4,21-2. 42:8-9, 44:6-8, 45:21-24, 46: 9-11, 48:2-6).

Whenever I am reading the word of God, mostly this book of Isaiah, I see a proud God hitting His chest and declaring words of potency, words of power, such that sometimes when I see my father or any earthly man trying to speak so proudly I just laugh especially when I sense the spirit in their words.

The book of lamentations 3:37 says, "So child of God, if anybody, be it from your father's house and lineage, to the man on the street, has said a word concerning your life, as long as you are born again, God your Father (John 1:11-13) says to tell you,

"Who is he that saith a, and it cometh to pass, when the Lord commandeth it not?"

The next man is Noah in Genesis 5, 6, 7 and 8. This story is about a man who God called and told him that He was going to destroy the world with rain. Now you must understand that what Noah faced in his days is what the church is facing today.

In Noah's days, something was about to happen that had never happened even since Adam fell in the Garden of Eden, and what was it? RAIN (Genesis 2:5). Just like we have never seen anybody come down from the sky before. So to Noah and the people of his days, it was funny and strange but the Bible said Noah believed God and this made him to obey God's word of building an ark. Hebrews 11:7, 2 Peter 2:5. That is what people are doing today when we tell them that this world will soon come to an end.

So, because things are still going on and it seems like nothing has changed since the days of our fathers except the political system, they too, like in Noah's time, laugh at us and Peter in his days saw this and spoke about it before we were ever born in 2 peters 3:1-10.

The next person is Abraham in Genesis 11, we see him with his father and he and his father make a move to Canaan but somehow they stop at Haran and Abraham's father dies there leaving only Abraham. He was an old man of 75 years and did not know what to do because he did not really know why his father wanted to leave Ur of the Chaldees for Canaan. All he knew was that dad said "Boy, let's move down to Canaan" and the old 'boy' at 75 said "Yes sir." Now, the man with the vision isdead and Abraham is stuck. In chapter 12 God steps in and offers Abraham HIS plan for his life and for all of humanity and when you are 75, life begins to wear you out especially when you have not achieved anything at that age except to marry and even at that, you still have nothing to show for from your marriage.

But just when Abraham was about to give up or may have already given up hope God shows up and begins to show him his future and Abraham believed God and begins to pursue his future with God. There were times he began to doubt God in Genesis 15 and 16. His wife sold him a different plan from that of God's and because it seems like God's plan was taking too long to come to pass he consented to that of his wife and Ishmael was born. Like I said in the beginning of this book, your purpose is spiritual and must be followed and done with the help of God's spirit (Zech 4:6, 1 Samuel 2:9). You can never fulfil God's purpose with your sensual knowledge (Isaiah 42:9,1Corinthians 1:29, Ephesians 2:8-9).

While in chapter 17 God shows up again after another 13years of allowing Abraham to follow his own plans and ambition of trying to bring to pass in his life a spiritual word from God. We, like Abraham are very guilty of this. When God tells us something He wants to do in our lives, we begin to use our human mind in trying to bring it to pass and when it looks like it is about to work, all of a sudden we fail and instead of waiting on God to do it in His time. Forr in his time he makes all things beautiful. (Eccles 3:11)

And in chapter 15 God told Abraham that his children would go to a strange land and that they will be in bondage in that land for 400years but He will bring them out with a strong hand and also give the wealth of that land to his children (Chapter15: 8-21).

And all this happened just as God told Abraham it would. (Genesis 27, 28, 29, 30; Exodus14).

Now time will not permit me to talk about the sons of Isaac, Esau and Jacob, Joseph the son of Jacob, Moses, the judges, the kings of Israel especially David and the prophets.

All these men were told by God what their purpose on earth was and how by depending on God, they were able to fulfil their purpose. Some were told at an early age while some, in their mid-life and others in their old age. They were told what to do and how to go about it. It was not easy, but they kept on trusting God and counting Him faithful even in times of great troubles and great danger and even when men despised them and called them all kinds of names, they still kept on doing what God said to do.

To them, life had no meaning outside the purpose of God for their lives. And they were ready to let all go just to fulfil purpose. To them letting go of their ambition was nothing compared to following God's purpose for their lives, which was of great joy and great privilege and they humbly surrendered to his every command. Paul says in Hebrew 6:12:

> **"that you be not slothful, but followers of them who through faith and patience inherit the promises".**

In your purpose, everything you are and will ever do has already been prepared by God. What you will have is both power with God and favour with man, even up to those who will try to stop you are all in your purpose. The places you will go, the people to work with and how much you need to fulfil that purpose, up to the woman you will marry and how many children you will have are all in God's blueprint for your life.

All He wants you to do is trust him. But no matter their age, they were still able to move with God in their days to change the course of time and that is why God told Paul to write their names in the HALLMARK OF FAITH (Hebrews 11:1-39), verse 40 says:

> **"God having provided some better things for US, that THEY without US should not be made perfect."**

The safest place to find what
tomorrow holds for you is in the
word of God.

Chapter Three

The Early Believers

JESUS said in the book of Matthew 6: 9-10 concerning the Father's purpose on earth being done not just in your life but on earth. He says to pray this way "after this manner therefore pray: our father which at in heaven, hallowed be thy name. Thy kingdom come. THY WILL (HIS WILL NOT YOURS) be done in earth, as it is in heaven."

In God's plan for man from the beginning of time, before and after Adam fell in the garden, God never made plans for the wants of man but for his needs. 2 Peter 1:3 says:

> **"According as His divine power hath given unto us all things that pertain unto life** (physical things) **and godliness** (spiritual

things).

And how do we begin to enjoy them, he goes on to say"

> **"through the knowledge of Him** (God) **that hath called us to glory and virtue"**

If you are a believer, then listen because I am talking to you, but if you are not, what I am about to say and all I have been saying cannot be of any use to you if you have not given your life to God through faith in His son– Jesus. You cannot control your life according to God's purpose and according to His plan. Because it takes the help of the Holy Spirit to fulfil your God-given assignment on earth. Romans 8:14, John 3:3-8 and Ezekiel 36:26-32.

Long time ago God had planned how we (believers in Christ) are going to operate in these end times, so He spoke it out in the time of Joel the prophet saying in Joel 2:28-29:

> **"...and it shall come to pass afterward, that I will pour out my Spirit upon all flesh; and your sons and your daughters shall PROPHESY, your old men shall DREAM DREAMS, your young men shall see VISIONS."**

Peter also makes reference to this in Acts 2:16-21. Now, this was the day of Pentecost and the Holy Spirit had just been given to the disciples of Jesus in verse 1-2, and the men that came to Jerusalem that day were not only the Jews but nations of the world, (verse 9-11) who have chosen to worship the God of the Jewish people. That was why everybody heard them speaking their different dialects and this called for a course of wonder among the non-Jews for they said in verse 7-8:

> **"...and they were all amazed, and marveled, saying one to another, behold, are not all these which speak Galilaeans? And how hear we every man in our own tongue, wherein we were born?"**

You can see that even this scene that day at Pentecost surprised not just the Jews but also the visitors because it was the visitors that were saying how surprised they were, not the Jews. If my father's brother in the village suddenly begins to speak French to my father, now I tell you that not just my father but the whole family including his own children will think he has gone mad, because he has never left Nigeria and has spent almost all his life in the village. So when and how did the French words enter his mouth? Just as those non-Jews were surprised on that day at Pentecost, so will I be the day my uncle in the village begins to speak French.

But see what Peter says to the great multitudes in verse 14, it says:

> "...but Peter, standing up with the eleven, lifted up his voice and said unto them, ye men of Judea, and all ye that dwell at Jerusalem, be it this day known unto you, and hearken to my words: for these are not drunken as ye suppose, seeing it is but the third hour of the day. But this is THAT WHICH WAS SPOKEN BY THE PROPHET JOEL"   Joel 2: 28-29

Verse 17 says,

> "...and it shall come to pass"

> verse 38-39.

Peter ends this Joel's prophecy like this. Then Peter said unto them,

> "Repent and be baptized every one of you in the name of Jesus Christ for the remission of sins, and ye shall receive the gift of the Holy Spirit."

Verse 39 says,

> "for this promise is unto you, and to your children, and to all that are afar off, even as many as the Lord our God shall call."

Boy! What joy it is when you see the words spoken years

ago or to you by God come to pass. You cannot know what it feels like until you experience it for yourself.

So if you are born again and filled with the Holy Spirit, the first thing the Holy ghost should do in your life after speaking in other tongues according to Acts 2:2, Acts 10:44-46 and Acts 19:1-6, is the ability to see tomorrow (vision). Joel says the Holy Spirit will give you vision; that means, show you what you are supposed to do on earth. When Jesus met his disciples, the first thing he said to them was **"...follow me and I will make you fishers of men"** (Matthew 4; 18-19). When he saw Simon (later called Peter) he spoke words, that to Simon were impossible to ever come to pass because of Simon's present state in life, being:

(1) A man that could not make or keep his words- a reed- (meaning of Simon) He called him a stone (Peter) - which means one that is strong, decisive.

(2) A weak man. Luke 22:31-32, Jesus tells Peter, **"Simon, Simon behold Satan hath desired to have you, that he may sift you as wheat: but I have prayed for thee, that thy faith fail not: and when thou art converted, strengthen thy brethren."** This means Jesus prayed that Peter even though weak now will one day become a pillar to his brethren, and we saw it happen in Acts 2.

(3) You will betray me, was the third word Jesus spoke into the life of Peter in Luke 22:34 and it was fulfilled in verses 54-62.

(4). The last words spoken to Peter by Jesus of things that will happen to him was how and when he was going to die and the manner with which it will happen and his assignment on earth John 21:15-19 and Peter in talking about his death related it back to what Jesus had already told him in 2 Peter 1:14.

Another man in the New Testament to look at is Paul. He was a ruthless man and he persecuted the church in his days. From his own biography in Philippians 3:4-8, Paul talks about his life before he met Jesus on his way to Damascus were Jesus appeared to him on the way and rebuked him for persecuting his church and then told him what he (Paul) was born to do Acts 9:11-19.

From here you can see that even Paul thought he had been working for God all this time, not knowing that all he was doing were born out of his ambition to please God. Remember it takes the Holy Spirit to help you do God's work on earth. Even Jesus the Son of God could not step into his ministry without the Holy Spirit coming on him. John 1:29-34

So my brothers and sisters in Christ, if all these names I have mentioned to you could not do what they were born to do without the Holy Spirit, they could not rely on their intelligence/experience or even on who they knew, what makes you think you and I can do our assignment any differently. Even God needed the Holy Spirit before He could repair the earth in Genesis 1:2. Of Jesus, it was said in Hebrews 10:7-8:

> **"...a body have you prepared for me on earth, look, I come to do your will, O God - just as it is written about me in the scriptures."**

So come to think of it, if all these names I have mentioned to you could not do what they were born to do without the Holy Spirit, they could not rely on their intelligence/experience or even on who they knew, what makes you think you and I can do our assignment any differently.

Chapter Four

You and I

YOU have seen that it's possible to see your end from your beginning. And all you need to do is give yourself to the pictures about you that the Holy Spirit will show you. When Jesus was leaving this earth, He said that the Holy Spirit is yet to come, and that when He comes into your life He will:

1. Guide you into all truth

2. Reveal Me to you and not himself.

3. Not present his own ideas.

4. Be telling you what he hears from me.

5. Tell you about the future.

6. Bring me glory by revealing to you whatever He receives

from me.

Nothing happens to me that I do not have first-hand information about. This is not just for a few in the body of Christ, but for all that carry the Holy Spirit on their inside to enjoy. You can see the future. Amos 3:7 says, "I do not a thing on earth without first revealing it to my prophets." What God is saying is that before He allows anything to happen to you or your family or nations, He wants you to be the first to know about it. Genesis 18:17, Numbers 12:6-8

Believers just die anyhow, and family members with them even knowing nothing about it, they begin to blame God for allowing it to happen.

Now, ever since 1994 till date, everything that has and is and still yet to happen to either me or my family members, even up to who they were going to marry and also the church I go to was all shown to me years before. I will tell you how it started to work. In 1994 my father wanted me to go to the U.S.A but things were not working the way he planned and I just rededicated my life back to God after about 6years of broken fellowship with him because I first surrendered to him at a very early age in 1981.

So in 1994 when the preparations to go to the U.S was in progress, my best friend Iyke also just got born again, and he was making plans to travel. Then one day he told me that God told him he was going to travel and that God spoke through his younger sister through the gift of prophecy (1 Corinthians 12).

So I went to meet her to also prophesy or get a message from God for me as to whether I will travel. But she kept telling me to go meet God for myself. You must understand purpose: it is not your plans but His, so why not just relax and let Him. When I came back from Makurdi, having not been able to gain admission, and after what that boy told me, I spent 2years at home in my room and with books to help me grow. I read my bible through 7 times. Even though I was having a great time with God, I also was receiving hell from my father who would call me names. Also, things seemed to be working out well for my friends.

Back then my room was all I had or my church but if I happen to come out and see my father it was like me standing before the devil himself. My house was undergoing a spiritual warfare and I was the one God was using and you know that it is the army in the forefront that is easily attacked. And I can still remember then that God would give me a word that would restore my soul after all those insults from my father.

During those days I came across a book titled "Call on Me". In that book, the author made me see that it was possible to see the end of one's life from his beginning and the scriptures he gave me were: Jeremiah 33:3, 29:11,

Habakkuk 2:1-3, Joel 2:28-29, Romans 8:2629, 1 Corinthians 2:9-15. Also, add 1 Timothy 1:18 and Jude 24. This I did by praying in the spirit (tongues), 1 Corinthians 14:2-5, every day, and speaking this scripture until almost every week I would be shown future events. Then, I also heard a tape by Pastor Benny Hinn who also said that the reason the Holy Spirit was given to us was for us to see the future. I also listened to another tape by Kenneth Hagin called, "The Spirit of Seeing and Knowing", it was on that tape I heard him laughing in the Spirit and ever since then I laugh in the Spirit because while he was laughing in the Spirit, I placed my hands on the cassette player and boy, it (the anointing) came all over me. I have this friend, I tell her everything God has told me. I also have a cousin I confide in that manner.

Also, whenever I am in a situation I don't understand, I go to my book of prophesies and see what time in God's plan I am in. Many times, this my friend and I have had misunderstandings and our mutual friends would think our friendship was all over. But then sometimes God would show me/lay it in my heart through the inner witness, Holy Spirit, (Romans 8:16) that something is about to happen to our friendship. Then I'd go and tell this my friend. How it would work out would also be shown me and this also, I would tell my friend.

Why does he do this? So that no man will take the glory Ephesians 2: 7-8.

Sometimes, following the pictures of God, like Bishop Oyedepo will call them (visions) while Dr. Myles Monroe calls them (purpose), is not always easy because you may just want things to work out the way you want them to, but I will say to you over and over and over again, HIS WAYS ARE THE BEST.

See it like this: if someone was in an helicopter telling you where and where not to go, you will obey because you can physically see him and you know he can see things from his point of view farther and better, how much more God who has already planned your life even before your mum said yes to your father.

Visions are like previews of a coming movie you have never seen and after watching the preview, the movie gets your attention and interest. So the next day you go to the movie shop to order for the movie. You do this because you already have a previous information on a particular movie, unlike before when you would only go there because you were bored. But because you know what you want and the price of the movie cannot stop you from having it. There is a movie about you and the movie shop is in the Holy Spirit in Jeremiah 33:3 and 1 Corinthians 2:9-15. Why not stop by and get the movie about your life.

Psalms 82:5 says,

> **"...they walk on in darkness and all the foundation of the earth are out of course,**

> but I have said you are gods and all of you
> are children of the Most High but you
> shall die like men and fall like one of the
> princes"

When we cannot see tomorrow we begin to walk like men in darkness.

Tomorrow is beautiful if only we can see it and speak only that the Holy Spirit reveals to our spirit by faith regardless of the circumstances surrounding us. 2 Corinthians 4:13 says we should speak just as men of old did because we have the same spirit of faith that they spoke by.

Because, in the WAY of God's purpose for your life, you have never been there before, no matter your age or experience in this dark world

Chapter Five

Warfare

1 Timothy 1:17-18

PAUL in writing to Timothy, his son in the Lord (someone you got born again and then helping him or her to grow in faith) told him to make sure that the prophesies and the gifts he received through the laying on of hands by him and some other ministers should be used to fight spiritual battles.

Now let me explain what Paul was telling Timothy to do. 2 Corinthians 10:3-5, tells us that our war is not against flesh and blood (physical man) and that is where a lot of believers miss it. Like I told you about the way my father would treat me. My father was not the enemy - there was an unseen force working through my father to try to discourage me and make me look down on myself with self-pity, and then begin to disbelieve what God said about me even before my father met my mother. Whatever anybody says about you is their own opinion and God will not stop anybody from talking you down, but He already told you what to say when they try to talk you down - Isaiah 54:17b "and every- it means what it says EVERY-tongue that rises against you in judgement (**YOU**, not God, **YOU**, not your pastor, **you**, not anybody, you, trust is stronger than you in faith), but **you** shall cancel it, condemn it or return to sender".

In this world that God created, man was made to rule it by **his WORDS and his THOUGHTS**. God, in creating the world, spoke it to be and when the devil tempted Eve all he used were words (Genesis 3:13). Before Jesus was born, words were spoken to Mary and when she believed those words, the result was that a virgin gave birth. You are a virgin in this world because you have not done what you were born to do. When a girl has not being touched by any man or nothing has gone into her to defile her, she is called a virgin. You too have not been used as far as God is concerned, you are still a virgin to your purpose in life.

To God, even though Abraham was already old at 75, he was still a virgin because he had not been given out to his purpose. Only your husband can come and tell your family that their daughter was a virgin after the honeymoon and not before. So until you discover your purpose in God, you are still a virgin. DON'T DIE ONE, empty yourself in God's plan. Remember when the children of Israel were about to advance to the other side of the river Jordan, God had to tell them that the land they were going to is new to them because they had never been there before. So, He commanded Joshua to bring the ARK of God forward so that the ARK can direct them on their way. The ARK was the symbol of the Holy Spirit and that was where He used to stay in the old covenant. But under this new covenant, we don't need an ARK to go before us because the day you got born again, the Holy Spirit came to dwell within you, and that is why you need to put Him first in everything concerning your life and purpose on earth.

Because, in the WAY of God's purpose for your life, you have never been there before, no matter your age or experience in this dark world Romans 8: 14

Words rule the world whether in the spirit or in the physical. And it is better you know the right words to use in other to get the right results that you need in life. Either right or wrong words, you will get whatever you say.

In 1 Corinthians 2:13, Paul says whatever the Holy Spirit reveals to you from the heart of the Father, that only should you speak. Jesus says in Matthew 6:10. Say in prayer, "Thy will, plan, council, word, purpose be done here in my life on earth and in my family, school, business, marriage, as it is in heaven". Can you remember when Moses was about to build God's temple on earth in the wilderness? God told him to make sure he does it just the way it was shown him on the mount (Hebrews 8: 5). So when Paul was writing to the church at Corinth, he told them that their enemy is not man but wicked spirits in high places. So stop attacking your neighbour and begin to speak what the Holy Spirit has told you to speak.

Paul was telling Timothy to do what he (Paul) had been doing whenever the devil would come against him – he would just speak the word of God. But which WORDS? The **Revealed Word** of God, revealed to him alone. Like when Paul was on the high sea and the storm came against his ship, he did not read the Psalms, thank God for the Psalms, nor did he say the Roses. No, he told the men with him in the ship what was revealed to him by God and that was, "I must stand before Caesar just as God told me" (Acts 27: 22-25). So what has God told you concerning your life? With the words God tells you concerning you, **MAKE WAR WITH THEM IN EVERY SITUATION THAT FACES YOU IN THIS LIFE.**

Some times when you listen to some men of God like the late Benson Idahosa, Kenneth Hagin, Bishop Oyedepo or Pastor Chris, you always hear them say things as touching their calling like "God told me to go and make my people rich" (Oyedepo) "God told me GO" (Idahosa) "God told me to take his healing presence to the world" (Chris) "God told me to teach my people faith" (Hagin). Joel 2.1-11 talks about an army coming in this last days from the church and every one of them will take their rightful place and stay there and they will know what they are called to do and another man's work will they not pursue. It says:

> **"...everyone on his way and everyone on his path and they shall not break their ranks."**

People of God, the only way you can get the right result in life is to first know your purpose from God and use that information from God to wage war in the heavenlies. Matthew 6:10:

> **"...thy will be done on earth just as it is in heaven".**

This is the reason why you pray, to see **His will done and not our will**; because there is no result for your will in his plans and no reward will be given to any plan born from man because, man's plan has a curse on it already (Genesis 3-17-19).

There was a time Jesus was talking to his disciples about him going to Jerusalem and when he gets there the Jews will hand him over to the gentiles to be killed and he will rise again. All of a sudden, Peter that was praised by Jesus called him aside and began to discourage him about the plan of going to Jerusalem when he (Jesus) knew that he would die there. But instead of Jesus rebuking Peter he turned and spoke to someone you and I are supposed to address when we are getting discouraged in pursuing our God given purpose either by our family or friends, and that person Jesus rebuked was the devil himself - even though Peter was still standing right there with Jesus. Jesus told the devil something I love so much in Matthew 16:21-23, he said,

> **"...get thee behind me Satan, for you understand not the things of God but the things of man"**

What Jesus was saying using our today's language was, you can only stop the plans of men because you understand where it is coming from. Because, man is dust and his plans are born from the mind of dust, and you have been given power over anything born from dust (Genesis 3:14). But God's plans are far beyond your reach and you have no power or business with it. You may try to stop it or try to make it not to come to pass but you are too small and have no understanding how it works and you never will. But man's own, you sure do. (Ephesians 2:1-3, 2 Corinthians 4:3-4).

Purpose is powerful!

Do not waste your time on your plans, go get God's plan for your life NOW. The number one enemy stopping you from fulfilling your God-given purpose on earth is the devil. He was in the garden and he still is right now and the only weapon you can use against him is not some prayer books churches give you these days. You are only wasting your time with that or any kind of prayer meeting which in its rightful place is good, but the only and safest weapon you can count on no matter what is, **what God told you about you**. (1 Timothy 1:17-18)

When Jesus was confronted by the devil in the wilderness all Ye used against the devil was the word of God revealed to him and not the ones he leant or saw someone use to get his or her own victory but what was revealed personally to Him and Him alone Matthew 4. And when David was about to face Goliath, Saul the king, wanted David to wear his armour, but when David wore it, he was not used to it, so he had to put it aside and make use of that which he was used to; that, which he used to kill both the bear and the lion when they wanted to attack his sheep in 1 Samuel 17.

So, please go get your weapons of warfare from the One that brought you into this world to fulfil your purpose. One time in 1996 when the senior pastor of the church I attend was moving the ministry to the US, we had two all night meetings, and in one of those meetings God appeared to me and told me that my parents will not die until they receive salvation.

Some years later, my father was really sick that some people thought he was going to die, but then I would still come home to collect money for school. It went on for about three months until one day I called my cousin Nosa and told him if he could remember the prophecy that God told me concerning the salvation of my father, and while we held our hands to pray, the power of God came so strong in the room like you could actually use a knife to cut through it and all I said was,

> **"God you told me that my parents will not die until they receive salvation."**

That was all. And some few days later, he was healed. Paul told Timothy in 1 Timothy 1: 17-18, "with this prophecy and gifts MAKE WAR". (Isaiah 41:21, Isaiah 43:26)

Even from your own family and church, yes church, but like I will always say people only know the facts about you but they do not know the truth about you.

Chapter Six

God is Faithful

Numbers 23:19

IF you have been a good bible study student you will always come across these words in the old and gospel books of the bible, the words "**and it came to pass**". It's all over the Old Testament and also the four books of the gospel. What it means was there were some things God spoke through the prophets and maybe later (or some years later), it came to pass just the way He said it would. And so the writer when referring to that prophecy will write "**And it came to pass**" (Acts 2:16-17).

Habakkuk 2:1-3, says about the vision,

> "**...it may take time to come to pass, but wait for it, for it will not take too long a**

time to come to pass, so wait for it."

Sometimes, we want God to quickly bring to pass all the things He spoke about us and we want them right now. Even though you were your father's first son and your dad is a multi-billionaire and you know that you are the heir to his empire and he loves you so much, but you are just 10 years old, that does not still entitle you to any decision making in the empire. You must first prove that you can be trusted before your father can then begin to allow you into some few things about the company and the things you will be told will be based on how much trust you have shown and how mature you are based on the things you can and have handled.

Only a foolish father will give his ten years old son his Swiss account books and documents to hold. Your life and purpose to God is very sensitive to His kingdom, so He has to make sure that you are mature enough to handle life's situations before He can begin to let you enter the pictures He had showed you about your life. Before then, you must go through some hard times (wilderness experience), so that the you that is ambitious and weak to handle heaven's assignment must first die (unless a grain of seed falls to the ground and dies its abides alone) for the you that you saw in the vision to come out. And maybe the you right now has so much flaws and hidden sins, a greedy man, proud, arrogant in nature, whatever, or maybe there are some habits you have been praying to God to deliver you from and some you may not see as one ONLY God can see it. So to get all these out of the way, God has to hold the vision until you are ready and strong enough to take your place in His plans for your life. And when you see that things are not just working out the way you planned them, don't worry or get angry with anybody or with God. Even when relationships are not going as planned don't complain, just say, "Lord let Your will be done just as it is in heaven." For the book of Ephesians 1:11b says,

"He worketh all things according to the counsel of His own will."

Galatians 4:1 and Romans 8:29

You will cry because of the pains you feel, the hurts you will get and shame you will bring to yourself, and this is when the devil would want you to give up the vision, this is when he would want you to curse God like Job`s wife told him to (Job 2:9). And this is when people will talk bad and call you names and even friends you love will lose hope in you and say you can never amount to anything in life. Even from your own family and church. Yes, church.

Only Truth Counts

Like I will always say, **People only know the facts about you but they do not know the truth about you**. Because I know the facts about a product does not make me the manufacturer of the product. Because I drive a Nissan car does not mean I own a Nissan Company and that does not also mean that I can talk for the company even if I work there. The only person that can and has the right to talk and defend the company is the MD or CEO of the company.

So also, because people have been with you and around you for a long time, and have seen your strengths and weaknesses does not make them really know you. All they have is facts about you. And in heaven, facts don't count, **ONLY TRUTH**. On earth, we address issues based on facts but before God, **truth** stands.

Go for the truth about your life and forget the facts, because when people see you, all they see is the facts (past and present) but your true you (future) is yet to come and that is why the pictures God shows you are about the true you that eyes have not seen nor ears heard, nor has entered into the hearts of man what God has made you to be and do (1 Corinthians 2:9). And verse 13 of 1 Corinthians 2 says you should only focus on the truth you and speak what the Holy Spirit has shown you.

Stop looking back; look forward into the picture of what God has shown you about you, your family, and your assignment on earth. You cannot be driving on the high way and be looking at your rear-view mirror, you will have an accident and die. So why die in the facts about you when the truth is yet to be seen and read about you in history? You are too much for this world or the devil or the facts about you. **Wake up to your truth**. Romans 3:3 says:

> **"...let God be true and every man that has called you names or looked down on you or turned their backs against you be a liar"**
>
> Isaiah 53:1.

Many people have died in the facts of their lives and many are living and seem to be doing well in the facts about their life but only the truth will make (not set, but make) you free. I come from a rich family so I know what pain it is when I see my dad always angry every day doing and living in the facts of his life. Oh, I don't care about the money or fame I just want to be happy and the only way to be, is for me to locate my place in God's purpose and plan for my life and then begin to pursue it no matter the shame (Hebrews 12; 1-2).

One day during our morning devotion with my father, we were reading Numbers 12, where God was angry with Moses' brother and sister for talking bad about Moses without him even knowing about it, and at the end of the meeting judgement came upon Miriam instantly and on

Aaron later. May God forgive us for talking about people we did not employ that are working for God, be it the pastor or a brother or sister no matter what they are doing because we don't know if it was God that told them to do it, **even if they make mistakes in Jesus name.** Amen. Romans 14: 4

So after the exaltation, my father said that that night he had a vision or a dream but he could not really place it, but what he saw was that I was talking like a lay man to a large group of people and they all loved what I was saying and when I finished, they were clapping. When he came to talk to them, all he said was that yes, I can talk but my handwriting is bad. Well after he told us that during the devotion I just took the good one and left the other one. Whether The President of the United States of America's handwriting is good or bad, it does not stop him from still being the number one president in the world nor does it affect the billions Bill Gates is making, nor does it stop healing from taking place in Pastor Benny Hinn`s crusade.

So, go for the truth about your life and let the world bother themselves with the facts about you. You are born for a purpose, you came for a reason. So go and make destiny happen in the name of Jesus and with the power of the Holy Spirit and based on the picture or truth about your life. Like Paul said to king Agrippa,

"I was not disobedient to the heavenly vision."

Peter also in 2 Peter 1:14, and Jesus in john 19:30. The late Archbishop B.A Idahosa once said during his last interview on air that I personally saw in 1995, he said and I quote "Everything God laid in my heart to do on earth, I have done". (1 Thessalonians 5:24, 1 Corinthians 1:9, Jude24, 1 Timothy 3:3, 2 Timothy 4:18) **YOU ARE TOO MUCH AND THE devil IS TOO SMALL FOR YOU.**

This is the reason why you pray to see his will done and not our will. Because there is no result for your will in his plans and no reward will be given to any plan born from man because, man's plan has a curse on it already

Chapter Seven

Declaration
of Faith

For with the heart, man believeth unto righteousness, and with the mouth, confession is made unto salvation

– Romans 10:10

ONE thing you must know and understand before you close this book is this – if you are not in fellowship with the Father by the help of the Holy Spirit, then you cannot experience what I have been trying to pass across to you.

In other words, you need to have intimacy with the Father

(your creator) and the Son with the help of the Holy Spirit. Only then can you begin to enjoy this life in the Spirit. You must be born again based on these scriptures: John 3:3-8, John 1:11-13 and Ephesians 2.

Thus, if you want to come into an intimate relationship with your creator, for only He can help you fulfil your purpose on earth, you can make this declaration of faith:

> "Father in the name of Jesus, I...................................... hereby declare based on these scriptures:Romans 3:23, John 3:3-8, Ephesians 2, that as a sinner, I need you, I need your assistance in order to function in Your purpose for my life. I believe in my heart the Lord Jesus and all that He came to do on the cross for me, and on the third day, He rose and is seated at the right hand side of God according to Ephesians 1:20.
>
> According to 1 John 5:10 -15, I .... believe the testimony of Jesus and openly confess with my mouth according to Romans 10:10 that Jesus is my Lord and personal savior, and because of this, I can now receive the baptism of the Holy Spirit with the evidence of the fruit and gifts of the Spirit and the

power of the Holy Spirit operating in my life based on Acts 1:8, Mark 16:16-18 and 1 Corinthians 12."

Now that you are born again, remember it is not your works but your faith that got you saved by simply believing in God's word.

Now you have a new life, new purpose, new focus and new plans – that are very different from the old ones you used to have. 2 Corinthians 5:17 says, "if any man be in Christ, he is a new creation: old things have passed away; behold, all things are become new." i.e. God does not reckon with your past, He relates with you based on the present.

Welcome to God's family (Ephesians 3:11).

The following scriptures will guide you in discovering your purpose in God:

2 Corinthians 5:17, Matthew 6:9-10, Proverbs 16:1-2, 1 Corinthians 2:9-15, Isaiah 46:9-10, Jeremiah 29:11,33:3, Romans 8:26-29, Jude 20.

> "Father in the name of Jesus, I............................... standing on these scriptures, need You to help me locate and

fulfill Your plans and purpose for my life. I also willingly give myself to the influence of the Holy Spirit to lead me according to Your plans and purpose for my life, and the Holy Spirit will guide me into all truth from the Word of God and show me things to come, according to Your word for my life. Thank You Father, for I know that from now on, all things are working together for my good, because I love you and because I am working according to Your purpose for my life in Jesus' name, Amen".

www.ingramcontent.com/pod-product-compliance
Lightning Source LLC
Chambersburg PA
CBHW051455150726
48000CB00005B/2401